IMAGES
of America

Remembering Mississippi's Confederates

On the Cover: In 1921, Confederate veterans toured the Harrisburg, Mississippi, battlefield and posed for a picture in front of a tree that was struck by a cannonball during the fighting. (Mississippi Department of Archives and History.)

IMAGES
of America

REMEMBERING MISSISSIPPI'S CONFEDERATES

Jeff T. Giambrone

ARCADIA
PUBLISHING

ISBN 978-0-7385-9413-2

Published by Arcadia Publishing
Charleston, South Carolina

Printed in the United States of America

Library of Congress Control Number: 2012938518

For all general information, please contact Arcadia Publishing:
Telephone 843-853-2070
Fax 843-853-0044
E-mail sales@arcadiapublishing.com
For customer service and orders:
Toll-Free 1-888-313-2665

Visit us on the Internet at www.arcadiapublishing.com

Dedicated to my wife, Jennifer, and daughter,
Sarah, who encourage and inspire me.

Contents

ACKNOWLEDGMENTS

This book was written with the generous support of the descendants of Mississippi's Confederate soldiers. The photographs and information they were kind enough to share with me have made this book possible.

INTRODUCTION

As a new decade dawned in 1850, Mississippi's future appeared bright. Twenty years earlier, the state had been a frontier, with a population of only 132,621. Indian cessions, however, opened up two-thirds of the state's land for settlement, and this proved to be a siren call to Americans seeking a better life. Men and women came by the thousands; between 1830 and 1840, the population of the state increased by an amazing 175 percent, the greatest rate of growth in a single decade in the history of Mississippi. From 1840 to 1850, the population increased another 63 percent, as more people immigrated to the state looking for wealth in the form of fields of cotton.

Not all of these immigrants had come to Mississippi voluntarily; by 1860, the number of African American slaves in the state was 436,631, larger than the number of free white citizens (353,901). The slave population of Mississippi was largely concentrated in the areas of the state suitable for large-scale cotton production: initially, the Natchez region, but after 1840, west-central Mississippi and the Yazoo Delta.

By the end of the 1850s, Mississippi was the leading cotton state in the country, producing over one million bales each year. In 1860, the value of Mississippi's farmland, implements, and livestock was nearly $250 million, and the state was ranked as the 10th wealthiest in the Union. To the citizens of Mississippi, it seemed like the good times would last forever . . . and then the war came.

Heeding the call of their state in 1861, Mississippians by the thousands left their homes and families to join the military and be part of the grand adventure to cement the independence of the South. Although the exact numbers will never be known, approximately 78,000 men from the Magnolia State served in the Confederate army during the Civil War.

Mississippians distinguished themselves on battlefields in every theater of the conflict. These men who fought so gallantly for their state were well motivated: they were defending their homes and way of life from an enemy they saw as a ruthless invader. But they paid a terribly high price for their service to country: some gave their lives on native soil, fighting at Corinth, or Vicksburg, or Brice's Crossroads. Still others found a grave on far-flung battlefields such as Manassas, or Sharpsburg, or Chickamauga.

The number of Mississippians who died during the Civil War is simply staggering. After the war, John L. Power, the former superintendent of army records for the state, made a study and concluded that 30 percent of the Mississippians who fought for the Confederacy died during the conflict. Of these casualties, 12,000 men were killed or died of wounds, and another 15,500 died of disease. The loss came to about one-fourth of the white males age 15 and above that had been counted in the 1860 census—an entire generation had been laid to waste.

Many of the soldiers who survived the war were left permanent invalids, having received terrible wounds that prevented them from supporting their families. Power estimated in 1865 that there were 300 amputees in the state needing artificial limbs, and advised the governor that $30,000 was needed to pay for the devices. The state legislature set aside $60,000 to pay for artificial limbs and to aid the widows and children of deceased soldiers. In 1866, it was estimated that there were 10,000 children in the state left orphaned by the war. Even those soldiers lucky enough to return home sound of limb faced an uncertain future. The harsh reality awaiting thousands of Mississippi soldiers in the spring of 1865 was summed up by Henry A. Morehead of the 11th Mississippi Infantry, who wrote, "It was too late to make a crop, and not a dollar except 'Confed,' not a bushel of corn, nor a pound of meat; nothing but a wife and child. So you see I was in the middle of a bad fix."

In addition to the human cost, the physical damage done to the state's infrastructure was extreme. Many of Mississippi's leading cities were left in ruins. A good example was the capital, Jackson. In 1860, it was a growing, prosperous home to over 3,000 people; in 1865, it was little more than a burned-out shell. On June 18, 1865, the *New York Times* reported on the town: "Once a beautiful city, it is now a mass of ruins. Piles of brick and mortar cover the once famous retreats of wealth and fashion. Numerous columns, shattered and charred, have suggested for the name of the place 'Chimneyville.' "

The economic losses in the state were just as great as the physical losses: in 1860, Mississippians had a personal wealth of over $351 million, and of that amount, $218 million was in slaves. In 1870, with slavery abolished, the personal wealth of Mississippians was only $59 million. In addition, 60 percent of the state's livestock was destroyed in the war, either killed or captured by the Union army. The few industrial establishments in Mississippi at the beginning of the war were largely destroyed during the conflict, and the state's railroad system was in terrible condition due to the damage it had suffered at the hands of the Union army.

Conditions certainly appeared bleak as the soldiers returned home in 1865, but these men were fighters, and the task of rebuilding all they had lost was a battle of a different sort. These Mississippians had been tempered by four years of war, and if there was one thing they had learned on the brutal killing fields, it was how to survive. And we, their descendants, owe them a debt of gratitude for the lessons they learned during the Civil War, such as fidelity to comrades, love of country, and courage even when faced with hopeless odds. These lessons were passed on to their children, and to their children's children, and have served Mississippians well over the years, helping them to withstand the very worst that either man or nature could throw at them.

This book is a tribute to the men of the Magnolia State who answered the call of duty from 1861 to 1865. They were truly Mississippi's greatest generation.

One

THE ROAD TO WAR

The 1850s was a critical decade in the history of both Mississippi and the nation. The land that the United States gained during the Mexican War brought slavery to the forefront of American politics. The Compromise of 1850 was supposed to settle the issue of slavery in the territories once and for all, but the rancor caused by the "peculiar institution" refused to go away. Issues such as the Kansas-Nebraska Act in 1854, the Dred Scott decision in 1857, and John Brown's raid in 1859 all kept slavery very much in the minds of Americans and widened the division between North and South. Mississippians were intimately involved in the politics of this era, playing an important part in the events that led to secession and Civil War.

Zachary Taylor was living on his plantation near the town of Rodney, Mississippi, when he was elected president of the United States in 1848. Although a Southerner, Taylor put the interests of the entire country ahead of those of pro-slavery advocates, which hurt his popularity in Mississippi. In the 1848 election, he lost the state to Democrat Lewis Cass by a vote of 26,537 to 25,922. As president, Taylor set off a fierce argument between Northern and Southern states in 1849 when he recommended that California be brought into the Union as a free state. A writer for the *Mississippi Free Trader* of Natchez blasted Taylor over his stand on California, saying, "He, General Taylor, President of the United States, for purposes of his own, undertakes to instruct these Californians in matters pertaining to their political welfare, and sends a pedagogue to teach them the alphabet of freedom." (Library of Congress.)

A native of Fauquier County, Virginia, Henry Stuart Foote was born on February 28, 1804. A lawyer by profession, he moved to Mississippi in 1826 and soon got involved in politics. Foote was elected to the US Senate, serving from 1847 to 1852, and during the debate over the Compromise of 1850 he played an important role in helping the legislation gain passage. At one point, the deliberation about the bill became heated, and Sen. Thomas Hart Benton of Missouri, who opposed the spread of slavery, walked toward Foote. The Mississippi senator, fearing for his life, brandished a pistol. On seeing the weapon, Senator Benton shouted, “Stand out of the way, and let the assassin fire!” Fortunately, cooler heads prevailed, and no blood was spilled on the floor of the Senate. (Library of Congress.)

Born in South Carolina on May 31, 1813, Albert Gallatin Brown moved to Copiah County, Mississippi, in 1823. Elected governor in 1843, he served two terms in the state's highest office. Brown was then elected to the US Congress, serving in the House of Representatives until his appointment to the US Senate in 1854. An outspoken defender of states' rights and an advocate of secession, in a letter to his constituents he said of the Compromise of 1850: "Can you, fellow-citizens, expect me to vote for it? Will you demand of your Representative to assist in binding you hand and foot, and turning you over to the tender mercies of the Free Soilers?" Brown resigned his Senate seat in 1861 when Mississippi left the Union. He organized and led the "Brown Rebels," which became Company H, 18th Mississippi Infantry. After serving briefly in Virginia, Brown resigned his commission in November 1861 when he was elected to the Confederate Senate from Mississippi. He served in this capacity until the end of the Civil War. (Library of Congress.)

John Anthony Quitman was born in Rhinebeck, New York, on September 1, 1798. He moved to Natchez in the 1820s, and was an enthusiastic supporter of his adopted state. A member of both the Mississippi House and Senate prior to the Civil War, he also served as a brigadier general of volunteers during the Mexican War. Elected governor of Mississippi in 1849, Quitman was an outspoken advocate of slavery, and pushed for the state to secede from the Union to protect her rights. In a letter to the Democratic Central Association of Mississippi in 1852, Quitman spelled out his views on slavery: "The result of many years of experience, observation and reflection, has also established in my mind the conviction that the subjection of the negro to the white race is in conformity with the designs of providence . . . this social institution, so far from being an evil, moral, social or political, is beneficial to both races, and has been, and now is, a chief element of the wealth, prosperity and power of these United States." (Library of Congress.)

John J. McRae was born in Sneedsborough, North Carolina, on January 10, 1815, and two years later moved with his family to Wayne County, Mississippi. A very popular pro-slavery politician, McRae served as governor of Mississippi for two terms (1854–1857). When congressman John A. Quitman died in 1858, McRae was chosen to finish out his term. On taking office, he promised to defend the institution of slavery, stating, "Mississippi has taken her position. I stand by that and know no one of all her people who means to depart from it. When it is violated by federal legislation, it dissolves the ties which bind us to the Union, and the federal power will be responsible for the breaking up of the government, not ourselves." (Library of Congress.)

A lawyer from Natchez, Mississippi, Robert John Walker served in the US Senate from 1835 to 1845. He was also secretary of the treasury in the cabinet of Pres. James K. Polk from 1845 to 1849. In 1857, Pres. James Buchanan appointed Walker governor of the Kansas Territory. Although a Southerner, Walker refused to approve of the Lecompton Constitution, a document designed by the minority pro-slavery residents of Kansas to bring the territory into the Union as a slave state. The governor had pledged that he would abide by the wishes of the majority in Kansas, and when President Buchanan upheld the legality of the Lecompton Constitution, Walker resigned in December 1857. When Mississippi seceded from the Union, Walker remained loyal to the United States, serving as a financial agent to Europe from 1863 to 1864. (Library of Congress.)

Jacob Thompson was born in Leasburg, North Carolina, in 1810. A lawyer by profession, he moved to Mississippi in 1837, and the next year was elected to the US House of Representatives, serving from 1839 to 1851. In 1857, Pres. James Buchanan picked Thompson to serve in his cabinet as secretary of the interior. While still in this post, Mississippi governor John J. Pettus appointed Thompson in December 1860 as secession commissioner to his native state of North Carolina. In a letter to Gov. John W. Ellis of North Carolina, Thompson wrote, "Wisdom dictates that all the questions arising out of the institution of slavery, should be settled now and settled forever." (Library of Congress.)

William Littleton Harris was a native of Georgia, having been born there on July 6, 1807. A lawyer by profession, he moved to Mississippi in 1837 and eventually became a judge. In 1858, he took a position on the Mississippi High Court of Errors and Appeals, now known as the Supreme Court of Mississippi. In 1860, Harris turned down a seat on the United States Supreme Court, believing that his adopted state was about to leave the Union. Appointed a commissioner to Georgia that same year, Harris spoke before the Georgia State Assembly, telling the members that it was his job, "To express the earnest hope of Mississippi that this state will co-operate with her in the adoption of efficient measures for their common defense and safety." (James Fox.)

Born on January 18, 1813, near Winchester, Tennessee, Reuben Davis moved to Mississippi in 1832, eventually settling at Aberdeen, where he opened a law office. Elected to the US House of Representatives, Davis served from 1857 to 1861, resigning when Mississippi seceded from the Union. In his memoir, Davis wrote of the reaction of his fellow Southerners in Congress when they learned that Abraham Lincoln had been chosen by the Republican Party as their candidate for president: "Lincoln's nomination took place about two weeks before adjournment. The intelligence came like a thunderbolt. Members from the South purchased long-range guns to take home with them. The unthinking among them rejoiced that the end was in sight, but those who considered more deeply were dismayed by the prospect." (Library of Congress.)

Two

The Gathering Storm

On January 9, 1861, the delegates to the Mississippi Secession Convention voted 84-15 in favor of taking the state out of the Union. After the Ordinance of Secession was passed, convention president William T.S. Barry cautioned his fellow delegates as to the difficult path they had set for themselves: "You have accomplished the work of destruction; but the courage, the thought, the wisdom, necessary to destroy are not always equal to the task of rebuilding. More is required in the future than had been in the past. . . . What lies before us will test the heroism, the higher, the nobler qualities of our race, inherited from revolutionary sires."

Once Mississippi seceded, thousands of young men flocked to recruiting offices to join the military. On January 23, 1861, the secession convention created the Army of Mississippi, but this organization was very short lived. With the creation of the Confederate States of America, most of the soldiers from Mississippi became part of their new nation's army.

The Mississippians who heeded their country's call did so for a number of reasons. Some went for excitement and adventure, others because they felt it was their duty. For the vast majority, the prime motivating factor was patriotism, which gave them a desire to protect Mississippi at all costs. Benjamin Humphreys, a planter from Sunflower County, who would become a general in the Confederate army, probably expressed the motivations of many of his fellow citizens when he wrote: "My nativity fixed my allegiance to Mississippi. Beneath her soil my ancestors and my children slept in death. All I held dear on earth, family, friends and property welded me to that soil by the strongest cement of nature. Her God was my God; her people were my people; her interests were my interests; her sympathies were my sympathies; I could not, did not deliberate after war was inaugurated and brought to her door-sills. I cast my lot with my mother state, and as she had crossed the Rubicon, I determined to march with her armies, whether her warpath led to Rome or ruin."

One of the richest men in Mississippi, Walter Leake Keirn of Holmes County was a delegate to the Mississippi Secession Convention. A staunch supporter of secession, he voted against amendments to keep Mississippi in the Union or even delay her departure. On January 9, 1861, he joined with the majority voting in favor of the Ordinance of Secession. (Mississippi Department of Archives and History.)

Lucius Quintus Cincinnatus Lamar served in the US House of Representatives, resigning in December 1860 to become a delegate to the Mississippi Secession Convention. After the formation of the Confederate States of America, he remarked, "Thank God! We have a country at last, a country to live for, to pray for, to fight for, and if necessary, to die for." (Library of Congress.)

Not all Mississippians were eager to see their state leave the Union. John Hill Aughey was a native of New York who moved to Mississippi prior to the war to serve as a Presbyterian minister. A very vocal opponent of secession, Aughey voted for a pro-Union candidate to the state secession convention, "Amidst the frowns, murmurs, and threats of the judges and bystanders." (*The Iron Furnace* by Rev. John Hill Aughey, 1863.)

James L. Alcorn was a delegate to the Mississippi Secession Convention from Panola County. An opponent of disunion, he tried to defeat or delay the Ordinance of Secession. When his efforts failed, he announced to the delegates, "The die is cast—the Rubicon is crossed—and I enlist myself with the army that marches on Rome. I vote for the ordinance." (Library of Congress.)

Representative Otho Robards Singleton resigned from Congress when Mississippi seceded. In a letter written to the citizens of Culpeper, Virginia, shortly before he left Washington, Singleton explained why his state had left the Union: "Submission to such dictation and insult is not a term to be found in her vocabulary. To her vision there float in the breeze but two banners—Upon the one is inscribed 'Disunion,' upon the other 'Dishonor.' Under the former she has ranged herself, prepared to take the consequences." (Library of Congress.)

Jefferson Davis was working in the garden of his plantation, Brierfield, just south of Vicksburg, when he received notice that he had been selected as provisional president of the Confederate States of America. His wife, Varina, wrote, "When reading the telegram he looked so grieved that I feared some evil had befallen our family." (Library of Congress.)

Before leaving Mississippi to be sworn in as president, Jefferson Davis told a crowd of well-wishers in Vicksburg, "I hope that our separation may be peaceful. But whether it be so or not, I am ready, as I have always been, to redeem my pledge to you and the South by shedding every drop of my blood in your cause." (Library of Congress.)

The inauguration of Jefferson Davis took place at Montgomery, Alabama, the first capital of the Confederacy, on February 18, 1861. In his presidential address, Davis gave this warning to the Northern states: "It must follow, therefore, that mutual interest would invite good will and kindness between them and us. If, however, passion or lust of dominion should cloud the judgment and inflame the ambition of these states, we must prepare to meet the emergency, and maintain, by the final arbitrament of the sword, the position we have assumed among the nations of the earth. We have now entered upon our career of independence, and it must be inflexibly pursued." (Library of Congress.)

Mississippi adopted a very distinctive uniform for its troops, as illustrated in this photograph of two unidentified soldiers posing with their muskets and bayonets. The state regulations called for a gray frock coat and pants, trimmed in red for infantry, yellow for cavalry, and orange for artillery. Headgear consisted of a black felt hat, looped up on three sides to form a tricorn. As if this was not distinctive enough, the enlisted men wore a horsehair pompon in their hats, and the officers had a plume in theirs. Although there was quite a bit of variation, many Mississippians went to war in 1861 wearing this uniform, and it will be seen in a number of the photographs in this book. (Library of Congress.)

After Mississippi seceded, prominent citizens often organized military companies for service in the war. A good example is James Gordon, a wealthy planter from Pontotoc. Gordon enlisted in 1861 as captain of the "Chickasaw Rangers," Company B of the Jeff Davis Legion, which he equipped at his own expense. In 1863, he resigned from the legion to become lieutenant colonel of the 2nd Mississippi Cavalry. (Janis and Forrest Tutor.)

This unidentified soldier is wearing what appears to be a Mississippi tricorn hat and is armed with either a Maynard carbine or a rifle. A breechloading single-shot weapon, the Maynard was known for its reliability and ease of use in combat. The state of Mississippi purchased 800 of the guns in December 1860. (Library of Congress.)

Due to shortages of uniforms and equipment in the early days of the conflict, many men marched off to war in civilian clothes, carrying whatever weapons they could lay their hands on. The two well-dressed soldiers in the photograph at right are armed with shotguns. In the picture below, James Thomas Asbury Cartwright, a member of the "J.W. Thompson Invincibles," Company E, 23rd Mississippi Infantry, is also dressed in civilian clothes and is armed with an artillery short sword. The sign on the table next to him, "Jeff Davis and the South!," marks this photograph as the work of an unknown photographer who was plying his trade in Corinth, Mississippi, in 1861. (Right, Library of Congress; below, Shirley McKenzie.)

Some of the first military companies to leave Mississippi were sent to Pensacola, Florida, in March 1861. Photographer J.D. Edwards of New Orleans took this photograph of soldiers from the "Home Guards," Company B, 9th Mississippi Infantry, in camp at Pensacola. The men are, from left to right, James Pegues, Kinloch Falconer, John Fennell, James Cunningham, Thomas W. Falconer, James Simms, and John T. Smith. The man standing in the back is unidentified. (Library of Congress.)

Kinloch Falconer was a newspaper editor in Holly Springs, Mississippi, before joining the army. His talents marked him for promotion, and he eventually became a major, serving as assistant adjutant general for the Army of Tennessee. Falconer survived the war, only to die in a yellow fever epidemic in 1878. (Terry Baker.)

Thomas B. Webber belonged to the "Jeff Davis Rifles," Company D, 9th Mississippi Infantry. Sent to Pensacola, Florida, the 9th participated in the Battle of Santa Rosa Island on October 8, 1861. Webber's brother, Watkins, was killed in the fighting, and Thomas took the body home for burial. He then deserted the 9th Mississippi and joined the 2nd Kentucky Cavalry, eventually rising to major in the regiment. (Brendan Mackie.)

John A. Moore enlisted in the "Meridian Invincibles," Company H, 14th Mississippi Infantry, on May 29, 1861. In this early war photograph, he sports a tricorn hat decorated with what appears to be a secession cockade, a patriotic symbol worn by many Southerners in 1861. Moore first served as a musician, and later as a sergeant, in his regiment. He was captured twice during the war, the first time at Fort Donelson, Tennessee, in February 1862, and the second time at Franklin, Tennessee, in December 1864. Sent to the Rock Island, Illinois, prisoner of war camp after he was taken prisoner the second time, Moore was not released until June 1865. (Jim Moore.)

Three

MISSISSIPPIANS IN THE ARMY OF NORTHERN VIRGINIA

In 1861, a number of Mississippi infantry regiments were rushed to Virginia to help defend the Confederate capital, Richmond. These units would be some of the first from Mississippi to see combat, fighting in the Battle of First Manassas on July 21, 1861. Five regiments fought at First Manassas: the 2nd, 11th, 13th, 17th, and 18th Mississippi. By the end of the year, there were another five units from the state serving in Virginia: the 12th, 16th, 19th, and 21st Infantry Regiments and the 2nd Mississippi Infantry Battalion. In the summer of 1862, the 42nd Mississippi Infantry joined them, and the last infantry regiment to reach the Old Dominion was the 26th Mississippi Infantry, which was transferred east in 1864.

In addition to the infantry regiments from Mississippi that served in Virginia, there were two batteries of artillery—the Madison Light Artillery and the Confederate Guards Artillery. There was also one Mississippi cavalry unit, the Jeff Davis Legion. All told, approximately 16,000 Mississippians served in Virginia during the war.

The Army of Northern Virginia was the principal eastern army of the Confederacy, and because of its long string of victories it was easily the most famous of all the rebel armies. Although this army wasn't officially organized until 1862, it had its origins in the armies created around Richmond in 1861. The Mississippians who fought with the Army of Northern Virginia served under one of the best leaders that the war produced: Gen. Robert E. Lee. Under his command, they earned their place in the history books, fighting in some of the most important battles of the war: Sharpsburg, Gettysburg, Chancellorsville, and the Wilderness. These men participated in some of the bloodiest battles of the war, and only 698 of them were present for the surrender at Appomattox in 1865. The rest of the 16,000 Mississippians who had served with the army, if they had not deserted or been discharged or transferred, were disabled, captured, or dead.

William Bryant Wooten of Panola County joined the army in 1862, after his older brother was killed in a skirmish with the Yankees near Holly Springs, Mississippi. He served in Company I, "Mississippi Reds," 42nd Mississippi Infantry. During the battle of Gettysburg, Wooten was wounded in the right hand, but was eventually able to return to his regiment. (Chris Marks.)

A farmer from Tallaloosa in Marshall County, Charles Burrow Best served as a private in "The Confederate Guards," Company G, 17th Mississippi Infantry. Severely wounded at the Battle of the Wilderness on May 6, 1864, he was never able to return to the regiment. (Bill Helbron.)

Edward Virgil Byron Maxey was a farmer from Chesterville, in Pontotoc County. He enlisted in the "Coonewah Rifles," Company H, 2nd Mississippi Infantry, on March 1, 1861, at the age of 19. Captured at Gettysburg on July 1, 1863, during the bloody fighting at the railroad cut, he spent the remainder of the war at the Fort Delaware prisoner of war camp. (Danny Honnoll.)

Joseph P. Owen (right) and his brother Glen Appleton Owen posed for this photograph in 1861 shortly after joining the "Confederate Guards Artillery," which was raised in Pontotoc County. The Guards were one of only two Mississippi batteries to serve in the eastern theater of the war, and Glen Appleton Owen was present at the Appomattox surrender in 1865. (Joe Mercer.)

Erasmus R. Burt was elected auditor of the state of Mississippi in 1859. He organized a military company at Jackson known as the "Burt Rifles," Company K, 18th Mississippi Infantry. Elected colonel of the 18th on June 7, 1861, Burt led the regiment at the Battle of Leesburg, Virginia, on October 21, 1861. Mortally wounded during the fighting, he died at the 7th Brigade Hospital in Leesburg on October 26. The first Mississippi officer to be killed in battle, Burt left behind a widow and eight children. A writer for the *Richmond Whig* lamented Burt's death, saying, "The 18th Mississippi regiment, his state, and the Country will feel keenly the death of Col. Burt. He fell in close action with the enemy, defending Southern soil and a cause that enlisted all his sympathies and energies. He was the model of an upright, honorable man—an experienced, intelligent and chivalric officer." (Trisha Borders.)

Josiah A. Lee of Desoto County served in the "Pettus Rifles," Company I, 17th Mississippi Infantry. At Gettysburg, Lee was badly wounded in the fighting at the Peach Orchard, hit in the shoulder and leg. Captured by the Federals, he was sent to the Point Lookout, Maryland, prisoner of war camp. Exchanged in 1864, Lee's wounds kept him from returning to his regiment. (Becky Lee Muska.)

Jeremiah "Jerry" Robinson, on the left in this photograph, of Port Gibson, enlisted in the "Sunflower Guards," Company I, 21st Mississippi Infantry, on July 2, 1861. He fought with the regiment in the battles of Savage Station, Malvern Hill, and Fredericksburg. Robinson was discharged from the 21st in December 1862 after furnishing a substitute to fight in his stead. (Beth Ballard.)

Born in London, England, Robert E. Scudamore immigrated to the United States in 1858, and eventually settled in Natchez, Mississippi. He enlisted in the "Natchez Fencibles," Company G, 12th Mississippi Infantry, in March 1861. Scudamore was wounded in the scalp and shoulder during the Seven Days Battles in 1862 and taken prisoner at Petersburg, Virginia, in 1865. (Allen Terrell.)

Thomas Mellard Barr was 17 years old when he enlisted on April 23, 1861. He served in the "Quitman Guards," Company E, 16th Mississippi Infantry, out of Holmesville, Pike County. Appointed a third sergeant in April 1862, he was badly wounded at the Battle of Sharpsburg, Maryland, on September 17, 1862. Never able to return to his regiment, Barr spent the remainder of the war as a hospital clerk. (Peter Miazza.)

At the Battle of Gettysburg, Brig. Gen. William Barksdale commanded a brigade consisting of the 13th, 17th, 18th, and 21st Mississippi Infantry Regiments. On July 2, his men smashed the Union line at the Peach Orchard before Union reinforcements stopped their advance. Barksdale was mortally wounded and captured in the charge, and his brigade suffered extremely heavy casualties. Of the 1,598 men who made the attack, 105 were killed, 550 wounded, and 92 went missing. (Library of Congress.)

Union army captain Andrew J. Russell took this unique picture at Fredericksburg, Virginia, in April 1863. He set up his camera on the far side of the destroyed Rappahannock railroad bridge, and some members of Barksdale's Mississippi brigade, who were quartered in Fredericksburg, proudly posed to have their picture taken. (National Archives.)

Captain Russell also took this picture on May 3, 1863, showing dead Mississippians of Barksdale's brigade shortly after their position along the Sunken Road was overrun during the Second Battle of Fredericksburg. (Library of Congress.)

Benjamin Grubb Humphreys planned for a career in the military, entering West Point Military Academy as part of the class of 1829. His new profession ended prematurely, however, when he was dismissed from the institution in 1826 for participation in the infamous "Eggnog Riot." In 1861, he raised the "Sunflower Guards," Company I, 21st Mississippi Infantry, and briefly served as its captain before being elected colonel of the regiment. Promoted to brigadier general after the death of William Barksdale at Gettysburg, he led the Mississippi brigade made up of the 13th, 17th, 18th, and 21st Mississippi Regiments until he was severely wounded at the Battle of Berryville, Virginia, on September 3, 1864. Sent back to Mississippi to recuperate, he was not able to return to his command during the war. (Library of Congress.)

William Henry Fitzgerald enlisted on June 25, 1861, as captain of the "Tallahatchie Rifles," Company F, 21st Mississippi Infantry. Promoted to major in 1863 and to lieutenant colonel in 1865, Fitzgerald led Humphrey's Mississippi brigade in the final months of the war and was captured at Sayler's Creek, Virginia, on April 6, 1865. (Beth Ballard.)

William Meshack Abernathy joined the "Mississippi Rangers," Company B, 17th Mississippi Infantry, in September 1862. He was badly wounded at the Peach Orchard in Gettysburg, on July 2, 1863. Captured by the enemy, he was eventually exchanged, but his injuries prevented him from returning to frontline service. Abernathy remained with the unit, however, and was paroled at Appomattox Court House, Virginia, on April 9, 1865. (John Hoopes.)

Harper's Weekly published this illustration of the 2nd Mississippi Infantry passing through Winchester, Virginia, on their way to fight in the Battle of First Manassas. The 2nd Mississippi suffered 25 killed, 82 wounded, and one missing in the first major battle of the war. (*Harper's Weekly*, August 3, 1861.)

William Harrison Pinson enlisted in the "Joe Matthews Rifles," Company D, 2nd Mississippi Infantry, on May 1, 1861, in Tippah County, Mississippi. Wounded in the leg at the Battle of Sharpsburg, Maryland, on September 17, 1862, he was never able to return to the regiment. (David Pinson.)

William Blake, shown in the left photograph, enlisted in the "Burt Rifles," Company K, 18th Mississippi Infantry, on April 4, 1862, when he was 17 years old. At Gettysburg, he was severely wounded in the leg and was left behind when the Confederates retreated after the battle. Taken to a Federal hospital, his left leg was amputated on August 11, 1863. After he recovered from his operation, Blake was paroled and sent back to the Confederacy. Despite his wounds, he continued to serve, taking a position in the commissary department at Mobile, Alabama. Shown below is the application Blake made to the Confederate government requesting that he be provided with an artificial leg. (Left, *1861 to 1865 by an Old Johnnie*, by James Dinkins, 1897; below, National Archives.)

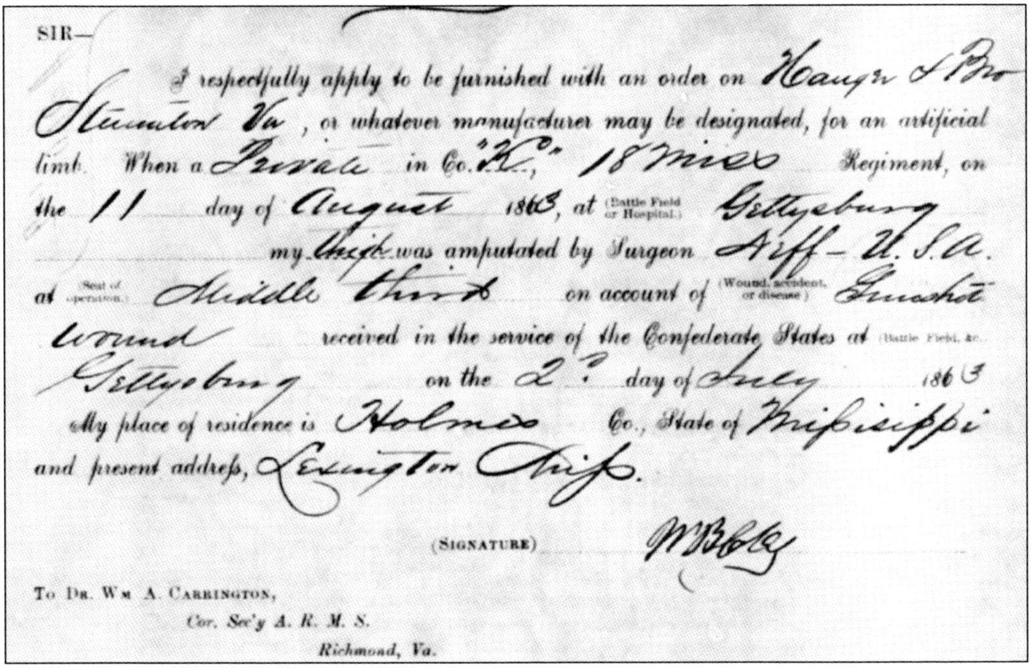

SIR—

I respectfully apply to be furnished with an order on Hanger & Bro Staunton Va, or whatever manufacturer may be designated, for an artificial limb. When a Private in Co. "K", 18 Miss Regiment, on the 11 day of August 1863, at (Battle Field or Hospital.) Gettysburg my thigh was amputated by Surgeon Neff – U. S. A. at (Seat of operation.) Middle third on account of (Wound, accident, or disease.) Gunshot wound received in the service of the Confederate States at (Battle Field, &c.) Gettysburg on the 2d day of July 1863

My place of residence is Holmes Co., State of Mississippi and present address, Lexington Miss.

(SIGNATURE) W B Blake

To DR. WM A. CARRINGTON,
Cor. Sec'y A. R. M. S.
Richmond, Va.

Nathaniel Harrison Harris of Vicksburg enlisted on May 14, 1861, as captain of the "Warren Rifles," Company C, 19th Mississippi Infantry. He advanced rapidly in rank, being promoted to major of the 19th in May 1862 and then to lieutenant colonel in November. Promoted to colonel of the regiment in April 1863, the next year he was appointed brigadier general after the death of Brig. Gen. Carnot Posey. Harris commanded a brigade consisting of the 12th, 16th, 19th, and 48th Mississippi Infantry Regiments; they were known throughout the Army of Northern Virginia for being hard fighters. Harris spoke highly of his men in his report on the battles of the Wilderness and Spotsylvania: "Thus during this arduous campaign of near ninety days, upon the field of battle and on the march, often using the pick and spade during the night, and the rifle all day, the men of this command have displayed these high qualities of courage, heroism, and endurance, that are the only sure indices of the tried and veteran soldier." (Library of Congress.)

Benjamin David Hennington enlisted as a private in the "Crystal Springs Southern Rights," Company C, 16th Mississippi Infantry, in the spring of 1861. In April 1863, he was promoted to lieutenant, and while fighting at the Battle of the Wilderness the next year, he lost his sword. Hennington survived the war and became a doctor in Lawrence County, Mississippi. In 1913, James R. Woods, who served in the 6th US Cavalry during the Battle of the Wilderness, put an advertisement in the *Times-Picayune* of New Orleans seeking to return to its rightful owner a sword he had picked up during the fighting. He was able to identify the Confederate soldier by the name and unit engraved on the scabbard: "B.D. Hennington, 16th Mississippi." Apparently, Woods was successful in his efforts, for Hennington proudly posed for this portrait holding his long-lost sword. (Larry Van Horn and Gayle Van Horn.)

A native of Germany, Simon Baruch immigrated to the United States as a young man. Wanting to become a doctor, he attended the Medical College of Virginia, from which he graduated in 1862. Baruch was appointed regimental surgeon of the 13th Mississippi Infantry in the summer of 1864. He was the father of financier Bernard M. Baruch. (*Confederate Veteran* XXII, December 1914.)

James Dinkins was born on April 18, 1845, in Madison County. As a teenager, he was sent to the North Carolina Military Institute in Charlotte, North Carolina. While a student there, he sat for this photograph wearing his cadet uniform. When the war started, he returned to Mississippi and joined the "Confederates," Company C, 18th Mississippi Infantry. A prolific author after the war, Dinkins wrote extensively about his wartime service. (*1861 to 1865 by an Old Johnnie*, by James Dinkins, 1897.)

James Alfred Conner, left, enlisted in the "Mississippi Reds," Company I, 42nd Mississippi Infantry, on April 21, 1862, at Sardis. Wounded at Gettysburg on July 1, 1863, he had to have several fingers on his right hand amputated. After a lengthy recuperation, he returned to the 42nd and was wounded again at the Battle of Weldon Railroad on August 18, 1864. In the postwar photograph below, a scar from this wound is clearly visible on Conner's forehead. (Bob Conner.)

William T. Martin of Natchez had a meteoric rise during the Civil War. He made a name for himself as commander of the Jeff Davis Legion, serving under legendary cavalry commander Gen. J.E.B. Stuart. Promoted to brigadier general and transferred to the Army of Tennessee in 1863, Martin ended the war as a major general, one of only five Mississippians to reach that rank. (Allen Terrell.)

Lt. Col. William H. Luse of the 18th Mississippi Infantry was captured at Gettysburg on July 2, 1863. Sent to the Johnson's Island, Ohio, prisoner of war camp, Luse escaped from the facility on January 6, 1864, only to be recaptured the next day. Eventually sent to Fort Delaware, he was released on June 20, 1865, after taking the oath of allegiance to the United States. (Library of Congress.)

Edwin Augustus Garrison lived on his parents' plantation, Ottawa, near Port Gibson when the Civil War started. He was very active in the Methodist Episcopal Church, and was licensed to preach in 1861. Garrison enlisted as a private in the "Claiborne Volunteers," Company F, 48th Mississippi Infantry. A note on this photograph states that it was taken shortly after he enlisted in September 1861 at Iuka, Mississippi. He was appointed first sergeant in November 1862. Garrison liked to preach to his fellow soldiers during his free time. One day, some officers overheard his sermon and recommended that he apply for the position of regimental chaplain. The young soldier did, and was appointed chaplain on May 24, 1863. Garrison served in this position until he was captured at Sayler's Creek, Virginia, on April 6, 1865. Sent to the Johnson's Island, Ohio, prisoner of war camp, he was released on June 14, 1865. (David Pierce.)

Pvt. William Barnabas Stevens enlisted in the "Vicksburg Volunteers," Company H, 48th Mississippi Infantry, in March 1862. He was killed at the Battle of Beaver Dam Creek, Virginia, on June 26, 1862. Stevens left behind a widow and four sons, the youngest of whom was only a few weeks old. (David Hoxie.)

James M. Tynes enlisted in the "Jake Thompson Guards," Company K, 19th Mississippi Infantry, on May 26, 1861. Wounded on June 27, 1862, at the Battle of Beaver Dam Creek, Virginia, he had this photograph made while he was recovering from his injury. (Paul Russinoff.)

This early war image depicts three members of the "New Albany Grays," Company K, 21st Mississippi Infantry. In the center is James Blackwell, and on the right is his brother Nicholas Blackwell. The soldier on the left is not identified, but may be John Calvin Pruitt, the stepbrother of James and Nicholas. (Union County Heritage Museum.)

This unidentified private was a member of the "Jake Thompson Guards," Company K, 19th Mississippi Infantry. Most of the men in this company were from Itawamba and Tishomingo Counties, and they were some of the first men from the state to volunteer for military service during the war. (Library of Congress.)

Brig. Gen. Nathaniel H. Harris's brigade of Mississippians took part in some of the most intense combat of the war, at the Mule Shoe Salient on May 12, 1864, at Spotsylvania, Virginia. This picture shows the graves of Mississippians killed at the Mule Shoe and buried near where they fell. (United States Military Academy.)

Immediately after the war, five members of the "Volunteer Southrons," Company A, 21st Mississippi Infantry, posed for this picture with their regimental flag. Only two of the men are identified: John M. Collier (first row, left) and Austin A. Trescott (second row, center). (Beth Ballard.)

Before the 1864 spring campaign started, Gen. Robert E. Lee sent a special order to the Mississippi units serving in the Army of Northern Virginia, explaining exactly what they were fighting for. He told them, "Soldiers of Mississippi! It is with great gratification that the Commanding General announces to you the joint resolutions of thanks passed by the legislature of your state. It is a just tribute to that conduct which in every campaign and on every battle field of the Army of Northern Virginia, has won for you his highest admiration. He mourns with you your gallant leaders and brave comrades who have fallen. May you cherish their memories and emulate their deeds. From her wasted fields and desecrated homes, Mississippi calls upon you to vindicate her honor and achieve her independence." (Library of Congress.)

Four

Mississippians in the Western Armies

While the Army of Northern Virginia ably defended the Confederate capitol of Richmond, it fell to the troops serving in the western theater to protect the Confederate heartland. It was in this huge geographic area that the bulk of Mississippians in the Confederate army served.

By late 1862 and early 1863, most Mississippians in the west were serving in one of two organizations: The Army of the Department of Mississippi and East Louisiana, or the Army of Tennessee. The former had among its responsibilities the defense of Vicksburg, and is best known for taking part in the 47-day siege of the city from May 18 to July 4, 1863. Mississippi was well represented in this army; a departmental return dated March 31, 1863, showed the state had twenty infantry regiments and three infantry battalions with this command. In addition, there were three regiments, three battalions, and one brigade of state troops attached to the army as well.

The Army of Tennessee was also well represented with Mississippians; in an abstract dated November 22, 1862, there were fourteen infantry regiments and one infantry battalion from the state shown as attached to the command. In early 1864, the Army of Tennessee was heavily reinforced with troops that had been serving in Mississippi, creating the largest congregation of state units to ever serve in one army—33 regiments or battalions. Although they were rarely victorious, the Mississippians who served in the west established for themselves a reputation as tenacious soldiers who very ably defended their homeland during the war.

Abel E. McAlpin of Smith County enlisted in the "Yancey Guards," Company G, 37th Mississippi Infantry, in April 1862. He served during the siege of Vicksburg and was captured when the Confederate garrison surrendered on July 4, 1863. (Art McAlpin.)

Alexander William Thompson was a first sergeant in the "New Prospect Greys," Company D, 5th Mississippi Infantry. He was mortally wounded in the Battle of Franklin, Tennessee, on November 30, 1864. Taken to the home of the Dotson family in Franklin, Thompson died on December 23, 1864. A wife and three children survived him. (Rosemary Thompson Scott.)

A successful lawyer in Jacinto, Tishomingo County, Arthur Exum Reynolds was a delegate to the Mississippi Secession Convention, where he voted against seceding from the Union. Despite this, when war came Reynolds raised and organized the 26th Mississippi Infantry, and was elected colonel of the regiment on September 10, 1861. The 26th Mississippi initially fought in the western theater, and Reynolds, along with the regiment, was captured at Fort Donelson, Tennessee, in 1862. After being exchanged, the regiment fought in the Vicksburg campaign, and in March 1864 was transferred to Brig. Gen. Joseph R. Davis's brigade in the Army of Northern Virginia. Reynolds was wounded at the Battle of Weldon Railroad, Virginia, on August 18, 1864, and never returned to the regiment. (Library of Congress.)

Berrien Troup Belsher was a merchant living in Burnsville, Tishomingo County, when the war began. He enlisted at Iuka on August 20, 1861, as captain of Company D, 26th Mississippi Infantry. Belsher had a very short war; he died, probably of disease, in February 1862. His place of death is listed variously as Franklin, Tennessee, or Decatur, Alabama. (Carol Ann Henson.)

John W. Malore was a private in "McDowell's Company," Company E, Ballentine's Regiment of Mississippi Cavalry. He was captured in Arkansas on January 17, 1862, and sent to a prisoner of war camp at Alton, Illinois. Malore was exchanged at City Point, Virginia, on April 1, 1863. (James Fox.)

Marcellus Pointer, a resident of Holly Springs, enlisted in the "Home Guards," Company B, 9th Mississippi Infantry, on June 3, 1861. He did a one-year enlistment in the unit, and sometime after his discharge he began serving as a volunteer aide on the staff of Maj. Gen. Joseph Wheeler. The general was so impressed with his conduct that he requested Pointer be formally appointed to his staff as a first lieutenant and aide de camp, saying that the young man had "displayed great gallantry in many actions." Pointer was a member of Wheeler's staff until November 1864, when he was appointed lieutenant colonel of the 12th Alabama Cavalry. Wounded in South Carolina in February 1865, he was recuperating at home in Holly Springs when the war ended. (Terry Baker and David W. Vaughan.)

Richard A. Pinson enlisted in the spring of 1861 as captain of the "Pontotoc Dragoons No. 2," Company K, 1st Mississippi Cavalry. Pinson was wounded at the Battle of Shiloh, and after recuperating, was elected colonel of the regiment on June 10, 1862. He was captured at Selma, Alabama, on April 2, 1865. (*Reminiscences of a Mississippian in Peace and War* by Frank A. Montgomery, 1901.)

David Andrew McElwain enlisted in the "Citizen Guards," Company A, 2nd Mississippi State Cavalry at Ripley on December 15, 1862. He was taken prisoner at Ripley on May 21, 1863, and spent the remainder of the conflict in various prisoner of war camps. In 1872, McElwain moved to Texas, living to the ripe old age of 93. He died in the Texas Confederate Home on September 5, 1937. (Robert C. Green and the Texas State Cemetery.)

Some of the bloodiest fighting during the Battle of Corinth, Mississippi, took place at Battery Robinett, an earthen and log structure near the Memphis & Charleston Railroad. One Mississippi unit, the 35th Mississippi Infantry, was involved in the attack on Battery Robinett and suffered extremely heavy casualties: 32 killed and 110 wounded. This photograph was taken shortly after the battle ended and shows Confederate dead in front of Battery Robinett. (Library of Congress.)

Patrick N. Horton enlisted in "Patton's Company, Mississippi Boys," Company A, 37th Mississippi Infantry, on February 20, 1862, at Marion. Captured at the Battle of Corinth, he was exchanged and captured a second time at the Battle of Resaca, Georgia. Sent to Camp Morton, in Indiana, Horton was transferred to Virginia for exchange, only to die at Akins Landing in February 1865. (Phil Lacy.)

Douglas Hancock Cooper was born in Mississippi on November 1, 1815. During the Mexican War, he served as a captain in the 1st Mississippi Rifles, commanded by Jefferson Davis. In 1853, Cooper used his close relationship with Davis, who was then secretary of war, to be appointed US agent to the Choctaws in the Indian Territory. In time, he was named agent to the Chickasaw Indians as well. In 1856, Cooper organized a local militia among the Choctaw and Chickasaw, and when the Civil War started, he brought this unit into Confederate service as the 1st Choctaw and Chickasaw Mounted Rifles. His regiment fought in the battles of Pea Ridge, Arkansas; Newtonia, Missouri; and Honey Springs, Oklahoma. In May 1863, Cooper was promoted to brigadier general and put in command of a district in the Indian Territory. (Library of Congress.)

Christian "Kit" Hoover enlisted in the "Summit Rifles," Company A, 16th Mississippi Infantry, on April 20, 1861. In November, he transferred to the 1st Kentucky Infantry, but left that unit when he was appointed first lieutenant of the "Stockdale Rangers," Company I, 4th Mississippi Cavalry in August 1862. Hoover was promoted to captain in 1863 and commanded the Rangers until the end of the war. (Bill Shepherd.)

Pvt. Edmond J. Rutland enlisted in the "DeSoto Brothers," Company I, 29th Mississippi Infantry, at Hernando, on March 1, 1862. Captured at the Battle of Lookout Mountain, Tennessee, on November 24, 1863, he was sent to the prisoner of war camp at Rock Island, Illinois. Rutland died there of pneumonia on November 8, 1864. (Cary Delery, www.historicalshop.com.)

John W. Frazer was appointed to the United States Military Academy from Mississippi, graduating in 1849. He resigned his commission in 1861 and joined the Confederate army. Commissioned a brigadier general in May 1863, he was given command of the forces protecting the Cumberland Gap in Tennessee. Frazer surrendered his men in September 1863, and spent the remainder of the conflict in a prisoner of war camp. (Library of Congress.)

A Baptist minister before the war, Brig. Gen. Mark P. Lowrey led a hard-fighting brigade of Alabamians and Mississippians in the Army of Tennessee. He wrote of his decision to join the army: "Every man who could bear arms should rise up and stand between his home and the enemy, and he [who] would not do so was deemed unworthy to be called a Mississippian." (Library of Congress.)

Years after the war, Eliza Margarette Trimble had a photograph of herself made into the composite picture, above, with her first husband, John James Screven Smith, who was a first lieutenant in the "Darden Rangers," Company F, 1st Mississippi Cavalry. Smith was mortally wounded and captured at the Battle of Selma, Alabama, on April 2, 1865. He died at Wayside Hospital on April 10, 1865. According to family tradition, Eliza went to Selma immediately after the war to find her husband's grave, but was not successful. In 1867, Eliza married George Washington Trimble, who served in the "Darden Rangers" as a private. The couple is shown at right. (Margaret Smith)

James Hamilton Mayson was a lawyer in Marion County and served as a delegate to the Mississippi Secession Convention. He enlisted in the "Jeff Davis Sharpshooters," Company D, 7th Mississippi Infantry, on May 4, 1861. Promoted to lieutenant colonel in September 1861, he gallantly led his regiment at the Battle of Shiloh, April 6–7, 1862. (Martin Hegwood.)

Harry St. John Dixon was a private in the "Washington Cavalry," Company D, 28th Mississippi Cavalry. A student at the University of Virginia before the war, he was a member of the Sigma Chi fraternity. In September 1864, Dixon gathered together a group of his fellow Sigma Chi's and founded the Constantine Chapter of the fraternity, which met until the end of the war. (The Sigma Chi Foundation.)

James Ronald Chalmers began the war as the captain of the "Irrepressibles," Company K, 9th Mississippi Infantry, but soon found himself in command of the regiment when elected colonel on April 11, 1861. In February 1862, he was promoted to brigadier general, and shortly thereafter was given a brigade consisting of the 5th, 7th, 9th, and 10th Mississippi Infantry Regiments. At the Battle of Shiloh, he led his men in a series of attacks on the first day that battered the Union left flank. The brigade suffered heavy casualties in this assault—out of 1,739 men, 82 were killed and 343 wounded—but in the process they captured over 1,600 enemy soldiers. General Braxton Bragg was so pleased with the performance of Chalmers's men that he dubbed them "The High Pressure Brigade," a title they proudly carried for the remainder of the war. (Library of Congress.)

Hezekiah George David Brown of Copiah County was the younger brother of Mississippi congressman Albert Gallatin Brown. A graduate of the US Naval Academy, he resigned in the late 1840s and returned home to Mississippi. On September 1, 1861, he enlisted as captain of the Seven Stars Artillery. (Suzanne Brown.)

James Adkins was from Milport, Alabama, about 23 miles east of Columbus, Mississippi. On December 20, 1863, he enlisted in "Richards' Company," Company H, 6th Mississippi Cavalry. He was with the regiment at the Battle of Harrisburg, Mississippi, on July 14, 1864, when it suffered heavy casualties assaulting the Union position (13 killed, 46 wounded). Adkins was one of the lucky few to escape unharmed. (James Fox.)

James M. Miller was a sergeant in Company A, 3rd Mississippi Cavalry. The 38-year-old farmer from Vaiden enlisted on May 3, 1864, at Tupelo. He served with the regiment until its surrender at Citronelle, Alabama, on May 4, 1865. (David Stewart.)

James Wiseman Honnoll was a Methodist minister living in Tishomingo County when the war started. One of his parishioners wrote of how the young preacher decided to join the army when the Confederates evacuated Corinth in 1862: "He immediately rose and said, that retreat means that I must become a soldier." Honnoll served as a second lieutenant in "Yates Company," Company C, Ham's Regiment of Mississippi Cavalry. (Danny Honnoll.)

After graduating from Miami University in 1857, Ohio native James Parks Caldwell moved to Panola, Mississippi, where he took a job as private tutor to the children of a local family. He was a good teacher and eventually opened his own school in the community, but the coming of the war put an end to his educational efforts. He enlisted in Captain Hoole's Company, Mississippi Light Artillery, in the spring of 1862. Caldwell quickly moved up in rank, and became an ordnance sergeant for the battery. In the summer of 1863, he was promoted to third lieutenant and assigned to the Watson Battery, Louisiana Light Artillery. He served with the unit during the siege of Port Hudson, Louisiana; after the surrender of the garrison, he spent the remainder of the war in various Union prisoner of war camps. (The Sigma Chi Foundation.)

John Franklin Deloach enlisted in the "Wilkinson Guards," Company D, 38th Mississippi Infantry, on April 29, 1862, at Woodville. He served with the unit until it surrendered in Alabama in May 1865. (Holmes Sturgeon.)

John Ferrell Mecoy of Tippah County enlisted in the "Sons of Liberty," Company G, 34th Mississippi Infantry, in early 1862. He was appointed a second lieutenant in the company on March 17, 1862, and later that year resigned his commission because of ill health. (Melissa McCoy-Bell.)

John G. Yeiser enlisted as a private in Company L, Wirt Adams Regiment of Mississippi Cavalry, on November 13, 1861. Promoted to quartermaster sergeant in 1862, Yeiser must have been good at his job, for he was appointed a captain and assistant quartermaster on the regimental staff in November 1863. (James Fox.)

John Waldo Henderson of Natchez served as a lieutenant in "Breckinridge's Escort Cavalry," enlisting at Washington, Mississippi, on July 24, 1862. This independent company started the war as personal escort for Gen. John C. Breckinridge. It went on to serve as escort for Maj. Gen. Alexander P. Stewart, Maj. Gen. William B. Bate, and Maj. Gen. John C. Brown. (Allen Terrell.)

John T. Broome from Hazlehurst enlisted in the "Copiah Rebels," Company G, 36th Mississippi Infantry, on March 11, 1862. He served as a wagon driver in the brigade ordnance train, and while working in this capacity was captured in north Mississippi in the fall of 1862. Sent to a prisoner of war camp, Broome never returned to his regiment. (Melinda Holloway.)

Lake Erie Eiland enlisted in the "Noxubee Cavalry," Company G, 1st Mississippi Cavalry, on March 18, 1861, at Macon. Eiland served as corporal and bugler in the unit until June 10, 1862, when he transferred to Hagan's Regiment of Alabama Cavalry. (Margaret Smith.)

Maj. Robert C. McCay, left, was leading the 38th Mississippi Infantry at the Battle of Harrisburg, Mississippi, when a bullet to the head instantly killed him. His brigade commander, Col. Hinchie P. Mabry, later wrote to McCay's wife, Elizabeth, pictured below: "With feelings of deepest sorrow, I announce to you the death of your husband. . . . While nothing can atone to you and your children for his loss, it will be a consolation to know that he died nobly at his post. . . . None excelled him in devotion to his family, fidelity to his country, and gallantry as a champion in the glorious struggle for freedom." (Rob Mobley.)

Fairfax Washington of Handsboro, Harrison County, Mississippi, was the regimental ordnance sergeant of the 38th Mississippi Infantry. He was wounded and captured at the Battle of Iuka, Mississippi, and died on October 2, 1862. (Paul Russinoff.)

Monroe Pointer was a planter in Shelby County, Tennessee, when the war began. He enlisted in the 154th Tennessee Infantry, and fought at the Battle of Shiloh, where he was wounded in the neck. In October 1862, Pointer was discharged because of a weak heart. He moved to Mississippi, and in 1865, he was conscripted by the state and given light duty with the quartermaster corps. (Terry Baker.)

This composite photograph shows six of the Pittman brothers, all of whom served in "Marion's Men," Company F, 7th Mississippi Infantry. From left to right, they are Enoch, Richard, Daniel, Stephen, Charles, and Jesse. Of the six, two died of disease (Enoch and Charles), one was killed at Chickamauga (Richard), and two were wounded (Daniel and Stephen). (Louis Morgan.)

Preston Brent of Pike County was colonel of the 38th Mississippi Infantry during the Vicksburg campaign. During the siege of the river city, he was struck in the face by a bullet that passed through both cheeks. Brent took a silk handkerchief and ran it through the wounds to clean them. After the siege ended, he went on sick leave and never returned to the regiment. (Brent Vasseur.)

R.W. Roberson of Tippah County was a third sergeant in the "Blount Guards," Company A, 23rd Mississippi Infantry. He was killed in the Battle of Coffeeville, Mississippi, on December 5, 1862. The 23rd Mississippi suffered two men killed, fourteen wounded, and four missing in the fight at Coffeeville. (Richard W. Roberson.)

Samuel George Fitten Jayroe of Winston County enlisted in the "New Prospect Grays," Company D, 5th Mississippi Infantry, at Enterprise, on October 18, 1861. He was severely wounded in the hand at the Battle of Shiloh, Tennessee. Promoted to corporal after returning to the regiment, he was wounded in the foot at the Battle of Murfreesboro, Tennessee. (Jo Rhodes.)

Thomas B. Beall enlisted as a private in the "Madison Rifles," Company I, 10th Mississippi Infantry, at Canton, in June 1861. He advanced in rank quickly, and by August 1863 he was a major serving as quartermaster on the staff of Brig. Gen. William F. Tucker. Beall later served as quartermaster on the staff of Brig. Gen. Patton Anderson. (Library of Congress.)

Thomas E.D. Traxler of Brandon enlisted in the "Price Rebels," Company G, 39th Mississippi Infantry, on May 1, 1862. He was captured with his regiment when Port Hudson, Louisiana, surrendered on July 9, 1863. After being exchanged, Traxler returned to the regiment and was killed in action during the Atlanta campaign on July 2, 1864. (Edward Traxler.)

Thomas Littleberry Cooper enlisted as a sergeant in the "Leake Rebels," Company F, 33rd Mississippi Infantry, on March 21, 1862, at Carthage. Elected a third lieutenant in October 1863, Cooper was promoted to captain in November 1864 to take the place of Capt. J.W. Sharkey, who was mortally wounded during the Atlanta campaign at Peachtree Creek. (Tom Cooper.)

William G. Bryant was 39 years old when he enlisted as a corporal in the "Mississippi Volunteers," Company G, 45th Mississippi Infantry, on December 15, 1861. Bryant was stricken with typhoid fever in the fall of 1862, and died at a hospital in Knoxville, Tennessee, on October 27, 1862. (Union County Heritage Museum.)

William C. Mecoy of Tippah County enlisted as a private in the "Tippah Tigers," Company C, 23rd Mississippi Infantry, on August 21, 1861. He was captured with the regiment at Fort Donelson, Tennessee, on February 16, 1862. Promoted to corporal in September 1862, he went absent without leave in May 1863, and was captured by the Federals in Tippah County on June 24, 1863. Mecoy ended up in the Fort Delaware prisoner of war camp, and was released on June 11, 1865, after taking the oath of allegiance to the United States. (Melissa McCoy-Bell.)

Haywood William Cooper of Holmes County enlisted in the "Nelson Grays," Company G, 4th Mississippi Infantry, on August 24, 1861, at Grenada. He had the great misfortune to be captured three times during the war: at Fort Donelson, Tennessee, in 1862; Vicksburg, Mississippi, in 1863; and Nashville, Tennessee, in 1864. Cooper was paroled at Camp Chase, Ohio, in 1865. (Charles Purser.)

William James Ford of Marion County was 18 years old when he enlisted in the "Jeff Davis Sharpshooters," Company D, 7th Mississippi Infantry, on May 4, 1861. Ford was discharged on June 15, 1862, on a surgeon's certificate of disability because he was born with a clubfoot. (Annelle Saucier.)

William R. Hartsfield of Lafayette County enlisted in the "Pegues Defenders," Company K, 22nd Mississippi Infantry, as a second lieutenant in July 1861. Apparently, Hartsfield's abilities as an officer were not very good, for when he resigned his commission in 1864, his commanding officer wrote, "This officer will make a better private than he does an officer." (Mississippi Department of Archives and History.)

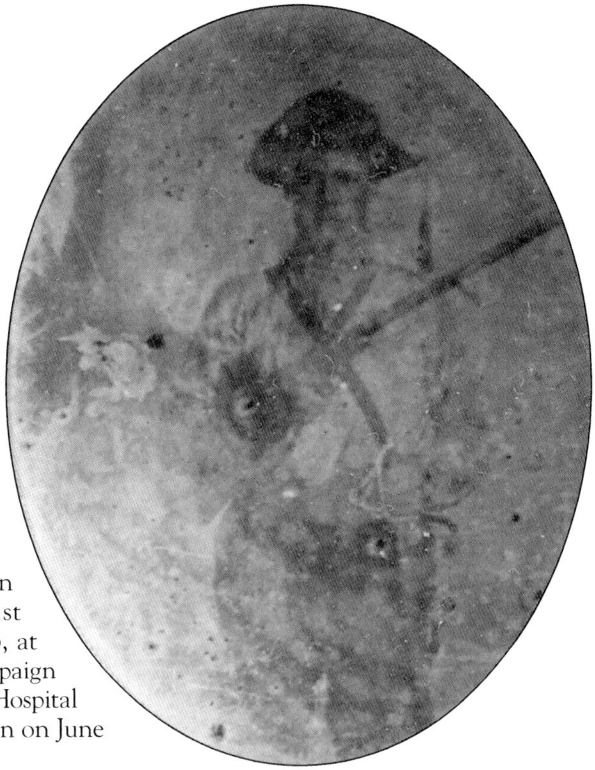

Willis Hunter enlisted as a private in the "Darden Rangers," Company F, 1st Mississippi Cavalry, on March 12, 1863, at Macon. Wounded during the Atlanta campaign in May 1864, Hunter was taken to Gilmer Hospital at Marietta, Georgia. He died of infection on June 13, 1864. (Margaret Smith.)

William Wirt Adams was a wealthy planter and banker in Jackson, Mississippi, before the war. He served as a secession commissioner to the state of Louisiana in 1861, and Pres. Jefferson Davis offered him the post of Confederate postmaster general. Adams turned down the offer and instead raised a regiment of cavalry. He enlisted on October 15, 1861, as colonel of the 1st Mississippi Cavalry. In December 1861, the secretary of war ordered that the unit be renamed Wirt Adams Regiment of Mississippi Cavalry. One of the best cavalry commanders that Mississippi produced during the war, Adams was promoted to brigadier general on September 25, 1863. He survived the war only to die in a gun battle with a political opponent in the streets of Jackson on May 1, 1888. (Library of Congress.)

W.S. Coleman enlisted in the "Dixie Boys," Company C, 24th Alabama Infantry, in 1861 when he was 16 years old. After the war he moved to West Point, Mississippi, and opened a hotel. In later years he lived in the Confederate veterans home at Beauvoir and served as chaplain at the facility. (Nancy Coleman.)

In July 1862, Capt. John G. Ballentine of Memphis, Tennessee, was ordered by Brig. Gen. John B. Villepigue, who was commanding in north Mississippi, to organize all of the unattached cavalry companies of that department into one regiment. Ballentine was named colonel of the new unit, known as Ballentine's Regiment of Mississippi Cavalry, which was made up of men from Mississippi, Tennessee, and Louisiana. (*Confederate Veteran Magazine*, Volume 24, 1916.)

Frank A. Montgomery of Bolivar County enlisted as captain of the "Bolivar Troop," Company H, 1st Mississippi Cavalry. Elected lieutenant colonel of the regiment on June 10, 1862, he served in this capacity until his capture at the Battle of Selma, Alabama, on April 2, 1865. (*Reminiscences of a Mississippian in Peace & War*, by Frank A. Montgomery, 1901.)

Pvt. John Burt enlisted in the "Clarke County Rescuers," Company C, 37th Mississippi Infantry, on March 13, 1862, at Quitman. Captured at Nashville, Tennessee, on December 15, 1864, he was sent to Camp Douglas, Illinois. Burt was released from the prison on June 18, 1865. (Emma Lou Burt Price.)

Pvt. John T. Thomas from DeSoto County served in Company D, 44th Mississippi Infantry. At the Battle of Franklin, Tennessee, he was wounded by a gunshot that fractured his right ankle. Thomas was captured in the battle and sent to Camp Chase, Ohio. He was released on June 11, 1865, after taking the oath of allegiance to the United States. (Neil Allen Bristow.)

Pvt. John Ross enlisted in Company F, 7th Mississippi Cavalry, at Pontotoc, on February 1, 1863. At some point he deserted the unit, for he was listed as "re-enlisted from desertion" on March 26, 1864. (David W. Vaughan.)

Lt. Samuel Wyles Johnson enlisted in the "Twiggs Rifles," Company L, 27th Mississippi Infantry, on October 2, 1861, at Pascagoula. He was wounded in the chest and captured at Lookout Mountain, Tennessee, on November 24, 1863. Johnson died in the general field hospital at Bridgeport, Alabama, on December 5, 1863. (Thomas and Dean Triplett.)

William Hockaday Brister enlisted in the "Rebel Avengers," Company H, 33rd Mississippi Infantry, on December 31, 1862, at Brookhaven. Apparently, the army did not suit Brister, as he deserted on April 25, 1863. He rejoined the unit in June, only to desert again during the retreat from Jackson, Mississippi, in July 1863. (James Catron.)

Thornton Hardie Bowman enlisted in the "Tensas Cavalry" from Tensas Parish, Louisiana, on February 28, 1862. This unit crossed the Mississippi River and became Company A, Wirt Adams Regiment of Mississippi Cavalry. Bowman was captured at Medon, Tennessee, on September 5, 1862, and exchanged at Vicksburg in November. After his return he transferred to Cameron's Louisiana Battery, and later was appointed a lieutenant in McNeil's Louisiana Cavalry. The left photograph was taken in 1864 while he was serving as a horse soldier. A fall from his horse in 1864 left Bowman permanently crippled, and he posed with his crutches in the below photograph, taken in 1904. (*Reminiscences of an Ex-Confederate Soldier, or, Forty Years on Crutches*, by Thornton H. Bowman, 1904.)

After serving as an officer in both the 15th Mississippi Infantry and the 29th Mississippi Infantry, William Felix Brantley was promoted to brigadier general on July 26, 1864. At the battle of Franklin, Tennessee, his brigade, made up of the 24th, 27th, 29th, 30th, and 34th Mississippi Infantry Regiments, suffered extremely heavy casualties: 76 killed, 140 wounded, and 21 missing. (Kenneth Brantley.)

Robert Herbert Conner enlisted in Company B, 9th Battalion Mississippi Sharpshooters, on May 1, 1861, at Pittsboro, Calhoun County. Wounded at the Battle of Chickamauga on September 20, 1863, he recovered and returned to his regiment. During the Battle of Atlanta, on July 22, 1864, he was severely wounded in the head and blinded for life. (Bob Conner.)

John Benjamin Wright enlisted in Company K, 45th Mississippi Infantry, on March 13, 1862, at Raymond. Wounded in the leg at the Battle of Murfreesboro, Tennessee, he was unable to march afterward and was discharged from the service. Wright later joined the cavalry and served until the end of the war. (David Hoxie.)

A native of Owen County, Kentucky, David Edwin Lusby enlisted in Captain Graves's Company, Mississippi Light Artillery, on September 7, 1861. Captured at Fort Donelson, Tennessee, on February 16, 1862, Lusby was sent to Camp Morton, Indiana. He escaped from captivity on May 23, 1862, and went on to serve in the 6th Kentucky Cavalry. (David W. Vaughan.)

An unidentified member of the "Moody True Blues," Company D, 8th Mississippi Infantry, posed for this picture with the initials of his unit on the front of his kepi. This company was from Clarke County, Mississippi, and was mustered into state service at Enterprise on July 17, 1861. (David W. Vaughan.)

One of the most popular commanders the Army of Tennessee ever had was Gen. Joseph E. Johnston. In the June 24, 1864, edition of the Meridian *Daily Clarion*, a reporter wrote, "Mississippi has between thirty-five and forty regiments with General Johnston's Army. After the battle is over our readers will hear of deeds performed by Mississippians that will be 'Chronicled in story and blazoned in bright gold.' " About that same time, Lt. Louis G. Sleeper of the 44th Mississippi Infantry wrote of the general, "The enemy had doubtless concentrated his entire force in our front. . . . Johnston seems to be making every preparation to welcome them to hospitable graves beneath the clod of good old Georgia." (Library of Congress.)

Five

Mississippi Veterans

Immediately after the war, Northern journalist Whitelaw Reid toured a number of former Confederate states, including Mississippi. He wrote of the attitude of white Southerners: "They expected nothing; were prepared for the worst; would have been thankful for anything. . . . They asked no terms, made no conditions. They were defeated and helpless—they submitted."

Only a few years after the war, Southerners started traditions designed to remember the soldiers who had died during the war. Confederate Memorial Day was established, and memorials to the fallen began to be built throughout the South. One of the first grave memorials in the South took place at Columbus, Mississippi, on April 25, 1866, when the ladies of the town decorated Confederate and Union graves at Friendship Cemetery with flowers.

By the late 1880s, Confederate memorial observances gave way to a more popular celebration of the war. Communities began erecting elaborate monuments, the most common being an individual statue of a Confederate soldier on a tall shaft, usually on the courthouse square or on a prominent street in the town. In 1908, at the dedication of a Confederate monument in Lexington, Holmes County, Thomas W. Smith, a former member of the 38th Mississippi Infantry, accepted the statue on behalf of all the local veterans. In his speech, he explained to the crowd the message that he hoped future generations would take from the monument: "It will speak in silent language to them of a citizenry and soldiery scarcely equaled, and never excelled, in any age."

In 1889, the United Confederate Veterans, an organization for former Confederate soldiers, was formed. It grew very quickly, and by 1903, had 80,000 members. In Mississippi, more than 85 percent of the counties in the state had at least one United Confederate Veterans camp.

Franklin Polk Gardner was 19 years old when he enlisted in "Buncomb's Fighting Cocks," Company E, 7th Mississippi Cavalry. In 1921, he returned to the Harrisburg, Mississippi, battlefield where he had fought as a teenager. Gardner had the photograph at left made with Ella Garner Smith, posing before an oak tree that was hit by a cannonball during the battle. Shown below is a close-up of the damage done to the tree when it was struck during the fighting. (Both images, Mississippi Department of Archives and History.)

Simon Mayer of Natchez was a member of Company B, 10th Mississippi Infantry, but spent most of the war as a clerk in the brigade headquarters. Recommended for promotion to major by Brig. Gen. William F. Tucker, Mayer was nicknamed "Too short to shoot," and the "Little Mississippi Major" because of his height of four feet, eight inches. (Allen Terrell.)

In the early 1900s, Confederate veterans from Port Gibson, Mississippi, took part in a local parade. The only men identified in the picture are James B. Allen (second row, left) and A.K. Shaifer (second row, right). (Mississippi Department of Archives and History.)

Thomas Clendinen Catchings, from Hinds County, enlisted in the Confederate army at the age of 14, serving first in Company K, 18th Mississippi Infantry, and later in Company C, 11th Mississippi Cavalry. Elected to Congress in 1885, Catchings introduced the legislation that created the Vicksburg National Military Park. Pres. William McKinley signed the bill into law on February 21, 1899. (Author's collection.)

Thomas F. Moriarty enlisted in the "Natchez Fencibles," Company G, 12th Mississippi Infantry, on August 2, 1862, at Brookhaven. He was taken prisoner at the Battle of Dan's Farm, Virginia, on the Petersburg & Weldon Railroad, August 21, 1864. Moriarty was sent to the prisoner of war camp at Point Lookout, Maryland, and exchanged on March 17, 1865. (Allen Terrell.)

Thomas Loring Lloyd served as a sergeant in the "Enterprise Guard," Company B, 14th Mississippi Infantry. He was captured at Fort Donelson, Tennessee, in February 1862, and sent to the Camp Douglas, Illinois, prisoner of war camp. Exchanged in the fall of 1862, Lloyd went back to his unit and was captured for a second time at the Battle of Franklin, Tennessee, in November 1864. Sent back to Camp Douglas, he was discharged on June 18, 1865. In this picture, Lloyd wears his Southern Cross of Honor and a ribbon for the Raphael Semmes Camp, United Confederate Veterans, in Mobile, Alabama, of which he was a member. (Alan Meyer.)

Born in Canada in 1841, Thomas Hunter moved to the United States in 1860 and ended up in the South. When the Civil War began, he joined the "Blythe Rifles," Company E, 44th Mississippi Infantry, on July 3, 1861. The regiment fought in the Battle of Belmont, Missouri, on November 7, 1861, winning the praise of Col. Preston Smith, their brigade commander. (Suzanne Paige.)

Walter N. Cooper enlisted in the "Burt Rifles," Company K, 18th Mississippi Infantry, on March 24, 1861. Shot in the chest and captured at the Battle of Sharpsburg, Maryland, he was eventually paroled but was never able to return to the regiment. Cooper died on his 84th birthday, December 5, 1925, in Crystal Springs, Mississippi. (Mississippi Department of Archives and History.)

William L. McMahon enlisted in Company H, 31st Mississippi Infantry, on March 13, 1862. Promoted to corporal in September 1863, McMahon was wounded at the Battle of Peachtree Creek, Georgia, on July 20, 1864, and sent home to recuperate. (Betty Copeland.)

William Robert Pate filed for a Confederate veterans pension in Texas in 1931 based on his service in "Company C, under command of Capt. McNeal." This may have been Company C, 1st Battalion Mississippi Sharpshooters. (Norris Long.)

Young Marion Langford joined the "Parrott Rifles," Company H, 40th Mississippi Infantry, on March 7, 1862, along with his brother and three nephews, all of Leake County. Langford was captured at Vicksburg in 1863 and again at Nashville in 1864. He and his wife, Elizabeth, moved to Texas after the war. (Ronald E. Wade.)

Francis Franklin Langford, shown with his wife and daughter, was the brother of Young Marion Langford. Francis joined the 40th Mississippi, but was soon discharged. He later joined Ham's Regiment of Mississippi Cavalry. According to the family, Langford was wounded in the war and walked with a limp for the rest of his life. (Ronald E. Wade.)

Isaac Hollingsworth enlisted in the "Yankee Hunters," Company D, 36th Mississippi Infantry, in May 1864, when he turned 18 years old. During the Atlanta campaign, he was wounded in the leg, but the injury was only slight. In 1907, he filed for a Confederate pension, stating that he was 61 years old and living with a daughter in Newton County. (Wren Harris.)

Alexander C. Abercrombie from Kemper County was first sergeant in the "Kemper Rebels," Company I, 5th Mississippi Infantry. He was wounded and taken prisoner at Missionary Ridge, Tennessee, on November 25, 1863. Eventually sent to Rock Island, Illinois, he was exchanged in New Orleans on May 23, 1865. (Peggie Hogan Moseley.)

Alfred Henry House of Natchez joined the "Natchez Rifles" on May 1, 1862. His company crossed the Mississippi River and joined a regiment from the Pelican State, becoming Company E, 4th Louisiana Battalion. Taken prisoner during the Atlanta campaign, House was held at Camp Douglas, Illinois, until the end of the war. (Dale Stewart.)

Allen T. Bowie of Natchez served as the adjutant of Wirt Adams Regiment of Mississippi Cavalry. General Adams wrote that Bowie was "a most gallant and efficient officer." (Allen Terrell.)

From 1877 until his death in 1889, Jefferson Davis lived at Beauvoir on the Mississippi Gulf coast. Sarah Dorsey, a family friend, left the home to him in her will. This photograph was taken at Beauvoir in 1884 or 1885. Seen here are, from left to right, Margaret Davis Hayes, Lucy White Hayes, Jefferson Davis, unidentified servant, Varina Howell Davis, and Jefferson Davis Hayes. (Library of Congress.)

Varina Davis, wife of Jefferson Davis, left the home Beauvoir, in Biloxi, to the Mississippi Division, Sons of Confederate Veterans, with the intention that it be used as a home for indigent soldiers. The first resident, J.R. Climer of Madison County, was admitted on December 2, 1903. This photograph showing the residents of Beauvoir was taken about 1930. (Mississippi Gulf Coast Community College, Claude & Avis Walker Collection.)

Benjamin Coulter Covington served in Company I, 2nd North Carolina Artillery, during the war, and was captured at Fort Fisher, North Carolina, in 1865. He moved to Mississippi in the early 1870s and settled in Lauderdale County. About 1910, Covington became a resident at Beauvoir, and this picture of him with his relatives on the front steps of the home was taken about 1916. (Martha Hutto Smylie.)

Joe Wiley (left) and Howard Divinity had their picture taken at the 1921 Confederate veterans reunion at Tupelo. Both had been slaves who went to war with their masters. Robert M. Scott, who served in Company D, 12th Mississippi Infantry, owned Divinity. In his pension application, Divinity noted that he had been wounded twice during the war. (Mississippi Department of Archives and History.)

The right photograph of Elias Oden and his wife, Annie, was probably taken in the 1880s. During the war, Elias had served briefly in the "Kemper Rebels," Company I, 24th Mississippi Infantry, before being discharged. He later enlisted in the "Farmer Boys," Company B, 35th Mississippi Infantry. Oden saw plenty of action with the 35th, being captured twice, once in north Mississippi in 1862, and again at Fort Blakely, Alabama, in 1865. Elias and Annie lived at the veterans home Beauvoir in Biloxi in their later years. In the below photograph, Annie poses with her grandchild on the steps of the Memorial to Mississippi's Confederate dead in Jackson. (Author's collection.)

The left photograph was taken while Frank Childress (left) and Nathan Best were residents of the Beauvoir Confederate veterans home in Biloxi. Both had been slaves who went to war with their masters. In addition to living at Beauvoir, each received a Confederate servant's pension from the state of Mississippi. In the picture below, Best's missing hand can clearly be seen. According to an interview he did with a Works Progress Administration worker, he lost the limb at Petersburg, Virginia, when a fall from a horse broke his arm so badly that it had to be amputated. (Left, Mississippi Gulf Coast Community College Dixie Press Club Collection; below, Jefferson Davis Presidential Library Collection.)

James Marks Tinnon posed for this photograph at his birthday party while living at Beauvoir veterans home. During the war, he served as the captain of the "Davis Guards," Company G, 33rd Mississippi Infantry. Captain Tinnon lived to be over 100 years old, and is buried in the cemetery at Beauvoir. (Jefferson Davis Presidential Library Collection.)

An Irish immigrant to the United States, Patrick McLaughlin settled in the South and fought with a Louisiana unit during the Civil War. Admitted to the Beauvoir veterans home in 1921 when he was 99 years old, he lived there until his death on August 24, 1925. This photograph was taken while McLaughlin was attending the 1921 Confederate reunion in Tupelo. (Mississippi Department of Archives and History.)

Thaddeus Lee Nichols served in the "Pettus Rifles," Company I, 17th Mississippi Infantry. In his later years, Nichols was a resident of the Beauvoir veterans home, and this picture was taken in 1931 while he was a resident of the facility. In the picture, he is writing a letter to Gov. Mike Conner, asking him to reconsider his decision to remove Beauvoir's superintendent, Elnathan Tartt. (Martha Malinowski.)

Thomas T. Pyron enlisted in the "Choctaw Planters," Company C, 30th Mississippi Infantry, on March 22, 1862. He was wounded at the Battle of Murfreesboro, Tennessee, on December 31, 1862. The doctors were unable to remove the bullet, and Pyron carried it for the rest of his life. After recovering from his injury, Pyron returned to his regiment and served with it for the remainder of the war. (Jim Kerin.)

William Tullie Bowie enlisted in the "Dixie Heroes," Company D, 30th Mississippi Infantry, on September 30, 1863, at Canton. In 1864, he was helping to build a breastwork near Resaca, Georgia, when the shell fired from an enemy battery caused a rock to fall on his foot, crushing it. Bowie's leg was amputated to save his life. In his later years, Bowie was a resident of the Beauvoir veterans home, and a small shelter was built for him on the grounds at the spot where he liked to watch the gulf. It was initially named "Bowie's Retreat," but the old veteran protested, saying, "Bowie lost a leg, but Bowie never retreated." The name was changed to "Bowie's Rest." (Mississippi Gulf Coast Community College Dixie Press Collection.)

Albert Gallatin Fore of Gulde, Rankin County, posed for this photograph on May 1, 1927, at the celebration of his 79th birthday. As a boy of 16, he joined the Mississippi militia to help defend his state. Fore is the author's great-great grandfather. (Author's collection.)

Mississippi governor Mike S. Connor posed for this photo with James W. Hazelett in the Vicksburg National Military Park on May 30, 1935. Hazelett was Warren County's only remaining soldier who served in the Vicksburg campaign, having been a member of the 28th Mississippi Cavalry. (Vicksburg National Military Park.)

James L. Kennedy enlisted in the "W.R. Nelson Guards," Company B, 32nd Mississippi Infantry, on March 6, 1862, in Lebanon, Tippah County. He displayed considerable talent as a soldier, rising from private to captain of his company in the span of just one year. (Edwin Kennedy.)

David B. Webb of Rankin County joined the "Rankin Greys," Company I, 6th Mississippi Infantry, by transferring from the 6th Mississippi Battalion on October 24, 1862. The addition of men like Webb helped the 6th Mississippi make good the terrible losses it had suffered at the Battle of Shiloh, where 70 percent of the regiment were casualties. Webb is shown in this photograph with his wife, Charlotte. (Norris Long.)

Charles Edward Hooker was a lawyer and member of the Mississippi legislature when the war began. He resigned his position and enlisted as a lieutenant in Company A, 1st Mississippi Light Artillery, on March 22, 1862. Wounded during the siege of Vicksburg, Hooker had to have his arm amputated. After recovering, he was promoted to colonel and given a position as judge advocate on the military court of Gen. Alexander P. Stewart's Corps, Army of Tennessee. After the war, he served for a number of years as a congressman from Mississippi. (National Archives.)

Long after the war, Edmonds Rivers Scruggs posed for this picture wearing his Masonic regalia. A member of Company D, Ballentine's Regiment of Mississippi Cavalry, he served as a lieutenant in his company and acting regimental adjutant during the conflict. Scruggs died on November 15, 1914, and is buried at Somerville Cemetery in Somerville, Tennessee. (Lura Wight.)

Isaiah Rush enlisted in the "Port Gibson Riflemen," Company C, 10th Mississippi Infantry, in September 1861. After his enlistment ended, he went home and then joined the "Van Dorn Guards," Company B, 38th Mississippi Infantry. During the siege of Vicksburg, Rush was wounded in the arm on June 18, 1863, and the limb had to be amputated. (Author's collection.)

When Jefferson Davis died in New Orleans on December 6, 1889, Southerners turned out in huge numbers to pay their respects to the former president of the Confederacy. In the photograph at left, 70,000 people viewed his body in state at the New Orleans city hall. On December 11, when his body was taken to Metarie Cemetery, 200,000 people lined the streets of the city to view the coffin. Shown below is the funeral car used to carry his coffin. In 1893, Davis's body was moved to Hollywood Cemetery in Richmond, Virginia, where it remains to this day. (Both images are from the Library of Congress.)

JEFFERSON DAVIS' FUNERAL CAR. NEW ORLEANS, DECEMBER 11TH, 1889

Stephen Dill Lee was a native of South Carolina and an 1854 graduate of the United States Military Academy. He was the youngest lieutenant general in the Confederate army, appointed to that rank in June 1864 to lead a corps in the Army of Tennessee. In February 1865, he married Regina Harrison of Columbus, Mississippi, and after the war was over he moved to her hometown. Lee led an extremely productive life in Mississippi, serving in the state legislature, as president of Mississippi A&M College, and as a member of the commission that helped to organize the Vicksburg National Military Park. He was commander in chief of the United Confederate Veterans at the time of his death. He passed away on May 28, 1908, in Vicksburg, and is buried in Friendship Cemetery in Columbus. (Library of Congress.)

John Henderson Freeman was a sergeant in the "Bowen Rebels," Company I, 34th Mississippi Infantry. Captured at Lookout Mountain, Tennessee, on November 24, 1863, he was sent to Rock Island, Illinois. He was paroled at Memphis, Tennessee, on May 25, 1865. In this picture, Freeman is wearing a ribbon with the words "Walthall's Brigade," and a badge from the 1904 United Confederate Veterans Reunion in Nashville. (Wanda Freeman Ridge.)

Matthew H. Bunn of Monroe County posed for this picture with his wife and children in the early 1900s. He served as a private in the "Buttahatchie Rifles," Company G, 41st Mississippi Infantry. He was wounded on August 26, 1864, near Atlanta, and his left arm had to be amputated. In 1890, he applied for and received a pension from the state of Mississippi because of his wartime injury. (Barry Bunn.)

Levi Tapp (right) enlisted in the "W.R. Nelson Guards," Company B, 32nd Mississippi Infantry, on May 1, 1862, at Corinth. He was captured near Atlanta, Georgia, on July 22, 1864, and sent to Camp Chase, in Ohio. Tapp was released on May 14, 1865. In the picture below, Tapp posed at the memorial to Gen. Albert Sidney Johnston at Shiloh National Military Park. (Ronnie & Michelle Huey.)

William F. Standifer enlisted in the "Raymond Fencibles," Company A, 12th Mississippi Infantry, on March 13, 1861, at Raymond. A prosperous farmer after the war, in 1904, the veteran decided to learn the latest farming techniques by enrolling at Mississippi Agricultural and Mechanical College. Standifer was a member of the corps of cadets, and posed for a picture wearing the uniform. (Mitchell Memorial Library, Mississippi State University.)

Charles Rudolph Martin (left) and Alfred Jarvis posed with the flag of their unit, the "New Albany Grays," Company K, 21st Mississippi Infantry. Martin was severely wounded in the leg at the Battle of Savage Station, Virginia, in 1862. Jarvis was wounded at the Battle of Sharpsburg, Maryland, in 1862. He was wounded a second time at the Battle of the Wilderness, Virginia, on May 6, 1864. (Jefferson Davis Presidential Library Collection.)

Roswell Belfield Willard of Amite County enlisted in the "Pettus Defenders," Company D, 12th Mississippi Infantry, on March 9, 1861, at Hazlehurst. He was discharged for poor health in December of that year. After his health improved, Willard joined a unit of sappers and miners who served at Vicksburg during the siege. (Barbara Slover and Ross Willard.)

John J. Lee served in the "Pettus Rifles," Company A, 17th Mississippi Infantry, along with his three brothers. A picture of his older brother Josiah A. Lee in uniform appears on page 35. John was captured at the Battle of Gettysburg after being detailed as a nurse to wounded soldiers. He was exchanged in February 1865. (Becky Lee Muska.)

Identical twins William James McIntyre (left) and John Sidney McIntyre were born in North Carolina but grew up in Tippah County, Mississippi. John moved to Arkansas before the war and served as a sergeant in Company H, 12th Arkansas Infantry. He was captured three times during the war. William served as a lieutenant in Company A, 2nd Mississippi State Cavalry. (Melissa McCoy-Bell.)

Eugene Houston Reber was a corporal in the "Rankin Greys," Company I, 6th Mississippi Infantry. He was discharged in May 1862, but later served in the Confederate commissary department. In his obituary, a friend wrote of Reber, "His good, manly heart was ever ready to alleviate suffering, ministering to the poor and needy often beyond his strength or financial ability." (Eric Pfeiffer.)

Survivors of the 22nd Mississippi Infantry met at Stafford Wells in Carroll County, Mississippi, on June 23, 1899, for their reunion. They paused in their celebration long enough to document the event with this photograph. (*Confederate Veteran Magazine*, Vol. VII, No. 9, September 1899.)

One of the best intelligence-gathering units in the Army of Tennessee was "Harvey's Scouts," named for its commander, Capt. Addison Harvey of Madison County, Mississippi. This photograph was taken at a New Orleans reunion in April 1906. The Scouts are, from left to right, Thomas B. Riggin, Hal H. Neal, Ike S. Harvey, Dr. Acy Gardner, Wallace Wood, William Sandidge, W.H. Howcott, and Wiley K. Nash. (Patrick Harrison.)

James Pinkney Cagle was the regimental bugler of the 11th Mississippi Cavalry. He is shown at left in a postwar photograph wearing his Masonic regalia. In the photograph below, he is shown at a Confederate veterans reunion holding a flag. (Dolores Stafford.)

Brothers James Polk Lofton (left) and George Dallas Lofton were both corporals in the "Chickasaw Guards," Company C, 31st Mississippi Infantry. The pair were both wounded in the left leg at the Battle of Franklin, Tennessee, on November 30, 1864, and taken prisoner on December 17 when the Federals captured the town. They were released from Point Lookout, Maryland, on June 6, 1865. (Morgan Gilbert.)

James Wesley McCluney served in Company F, 3rd Battalion Mississippi Infantry, State Troops. He was captured at Vicksburg when the city surrendered on July 4, 1863. McCluney later served in Company F, 6th Mississippi Cavalry. (Larry McCluney.)

A sergeant in the "Scotland Guards," Company K, 5th Mississippi Infantry, William Benjamin Brantley was severely wounded in the head at the Battle of Shiloh, Tennessee, causing him to lose his eye. He returned to the regiment after recovering, and was captured at the Battle of Franklin, Tennessee, on November 30, 1864. Sent to Camp Douglas, Illinois, Brantley was released in June 1865. (Kenneth Brantley.)

John Calvin Portis of Newton County was a private in the "Pinckney Guards," Company B, 8th Mississippi Infantry. Wounded at the Battle of Resaca, Georgia, on May 14, 1864, his right arm had to be amputated. In his obituary, a friend wrote, "An empty sleeve was his badge of valor and honor in his after life." (*Confederate Veteran Magazine*, Volume 18, January 1910.)

Henry Barlow Blackwell enlisted in the "Davenport Rifles" on May 14, 1862, at Booneville. He had the extreme bad luck to be captured by the Yankees before he could report to his unit, so his initial service was as a prisoner of war. Exchanged in the fall of 1862, Blackwell was wounded in the leg and captured a second time at the Battle of Gettysburg. (Hank Blackwell.)

John Marshall Eakin was in the "Singleton Guards," Company G, 46th Mississippi Infantry. Captured near Franklin, Tennessee, in December 1864, Eakin was sent to Camp Douglas, Illinois. To escape the dreary life of a prisoner, Eakin volunteered to serve three years in Company I, 5th United States Volunteer Infantry, on April 15, 1865. Sent to Kansas, he served until October 3, 1865, when he deserted. (Wanda Eakin Lentz.)

Winfield Scott Gibson was 85 years old when he posed for this photograph. He served in Company L, Wirt Adams Regiment of Mississippi Cavalry, and was wounded through the lungs at the Battle of Franklin, Tennessee. Gibson recovered from his wounds and returned to his unit. He surrendered with the regiment in Alabama in 1865. (Vicksburg National Military Park.)

The United Daughters of the Confederacy erected a Confederate monument on the main street of Amory, Mississippi, in 1924. Sometime thereafter, a local group of Confederate veterans posed for this picture with the monument. (Amory Regional Museum.)

Josiah Benson Dunn served briefly as captain of the "Wigfall Rifles," Company D, 15th Mississippi Infantry. He resigned in April 1862 because of poor health. Dunn is pictured here with his wife, Missouri, who was the sister of Gen. William F. Brantley. (Kenneth Brantley.)

John Bunyan Brown enlisted in the "Beauregard Rifles," Company F, 14th Mississippi Infantry, at Bowling Green, Kentucky. Captured at Fort Donelson, Tennessee, in February 1862, he was sent to Camp Douglas, Illinois. Exchanged in September 1862, Brown was discharged for poor health soon thereafter. After recovering, he joined the 11th Mississippi Cavalry in May 1863. (Beth Hemphill.)

James Dinkins, seen in a wartime photograph on page 45, was very active in the United Confederate Veterans. He is seen here, on the right, while serving on the staff of United Confederate Veterans commander George P. Harrison (center). On the left is William E. Mickel, adjutant general of the United Confederate Veterans. The picture was taken in Washington, D.C., in 1917, at the organization's annual reunion. (Library of Congress.)

Brothers Jacob Lewis (left), Willis Lewis (center), and Walden Lewis lost their father, Simeon Thomas Lewis, during the war. He was killed during the siege of Vicksburg while serving in Company A, 5th Mississippi Infantry, State Troops. Both Jacob and Walden were veterans themselves, having served in Company A, 1st Mississippi Cavalry, Reserves. (Charles Lewis.)

The members of the S.H. Powe Camp, United Confederate Veterans, posed for this picture at Waynesboro, Mississippi, in 1909. (Mississippi Department of Archives and History.)

William M. Weatherall was a drummer for the "Fredonia Hards," Company C, 27th Mississippi Infantry. He enlisted on July 25, 1861, in Pontotoc County, and was severely wounded at Resaca, Georgia, in May 1864. (Cindy Steinman.)

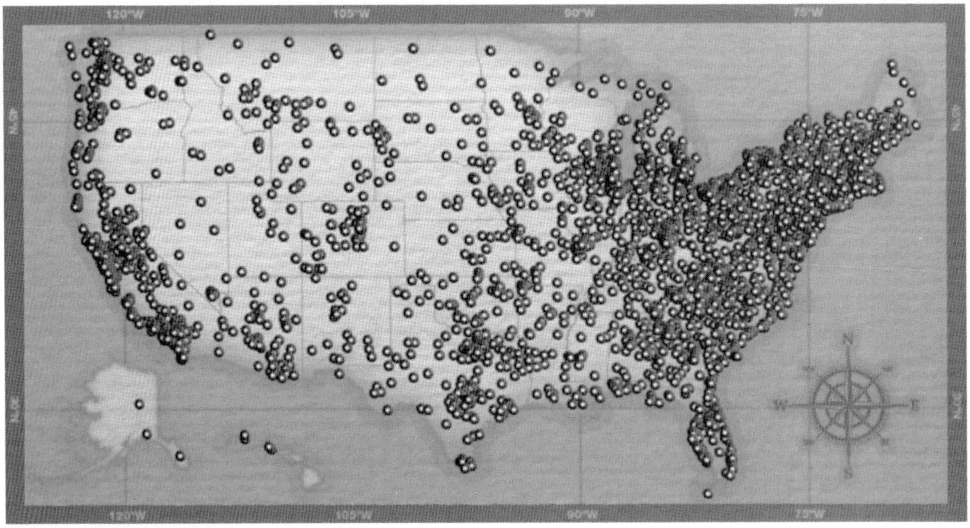

Consistent with our mission to preserve history on a local level, this book was printed in South Carolina on American-made paper and manufactured entirely in the United States. Products carrying the accredited Forest Stewardship Council (FSC) label are printed on 100 percent FSC-certified paper.

MADE IN THE USA